PERFECT OR PERFECTED

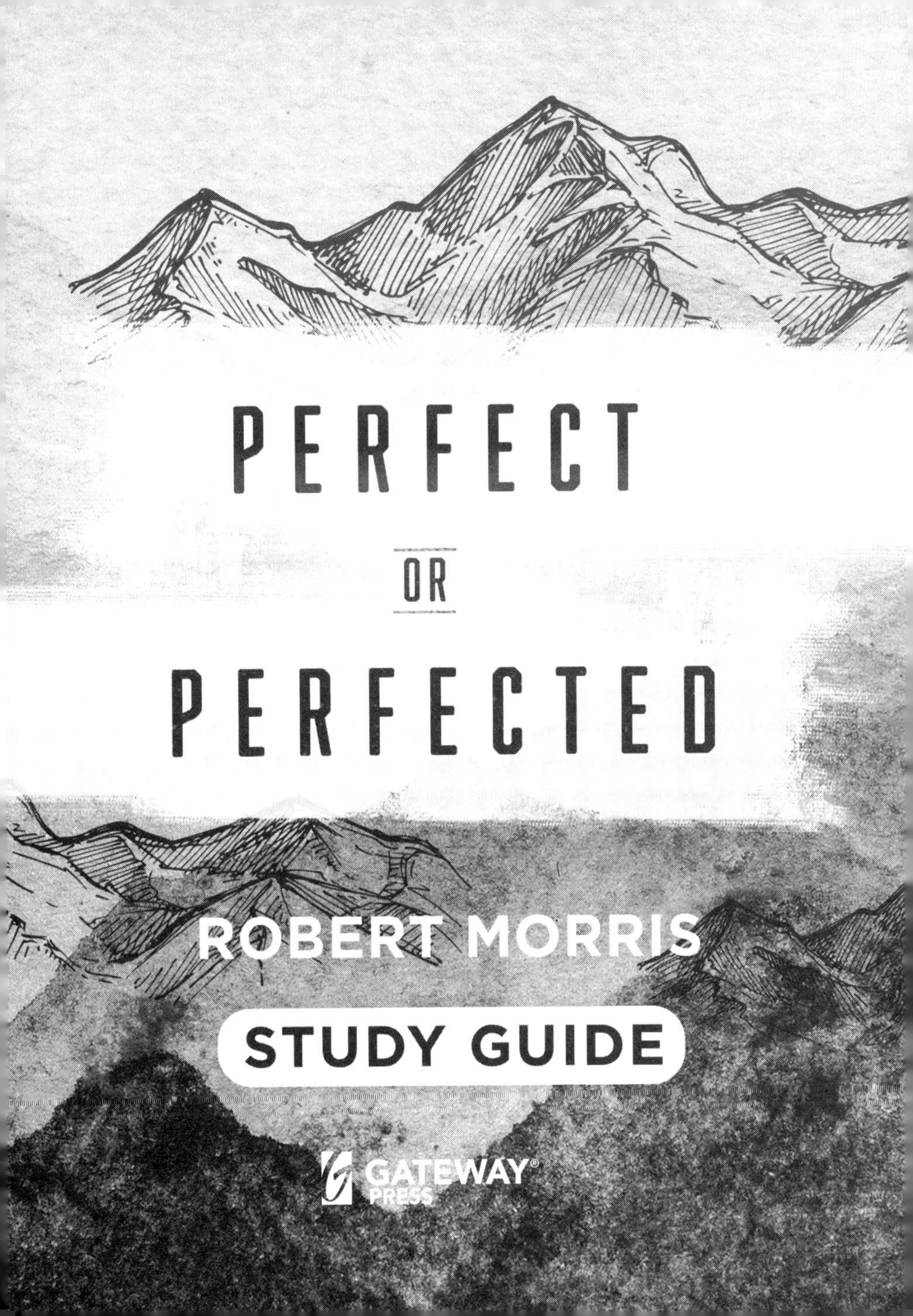

PERFECT OR PERFECTED

ROBERT MORRIS

STUDY GUIDE

GATEWAY PRESS

GATEWAY®
PRESS

Perfect or Perfected

Content taken from sermons delivered in 2020 by Robert Morris at Gateway Church, Southlake, TX.

ISBN: 978-1-951227-78-4 Paperback
ISBN: 978-1-951227-79-1 eBook
ISBN: 978-1-951227-80-7 DVD

We hope you hear from the Holy Spirit and receive God's richest blessings from this book by Gateway Press. We want to provide the highest quality resources that take the messages, music, and media of Gateway Church to the world. For more information on other resources from Gateway Publishing®, go to gatewaypublishing.com.

Gateway Press, an imprint of Gateway Publishing
700 Blessed Way
Southlake, TX 76092
gatewaypublishing.com

Printed in the United States of America

21 22 23 24 25 5 4 3 2 1

CONTENTS

1

PERFECTIONISM

All our efforts to be perfect fall short, but we can find hope in God's Word.

ENGAGE

What's the weirdest thing you do to be perfect? Straighten pictures? Remake the bed several times?

WATCH

Watch "Perfectionism."

- Consider how the word "perfect" is used in our society.
- Look for how God defines perfect.

(If you are not able to watch this teaching on video, read the following. Otherwise, skip to the **Talk** section after viewing.)

READ

This new series is called *Perfect or Perfected*. The word "perfect" is a buzzword today. When someone says, "We'll talk about this tomorrow," our answer might be, "Perfect." Or "How about lunch on Thursday?" Again, the answer is often, "Perfect." Some people I know use "perfect" all the time.

I'm Not Perfect

I'm using first person here, but I'm talking about all of us. When you think of this point, I want you to say, "I'm not perfect."

Merriam-Webster defines perfect as being "entirely without fault or defect."[1] I don't really need many Scriptures to demonstrate this point. Romans 3:23 says, "All have sinned and fall short of the glory of God." All. This Greek word for sinned is *hamartano*. Like many Greek words in the Bible, this word has a sporting context. It means 'to miss the mark.' It refers, in archery, to an arrow that doesn't hit the center of the bullseye. You can hit the target and just miss the center of the bullseye and not be perfect.

Perfectionism is an unreachable goal for humans. We still try, but it just causes us stress and worry. You can't do a perfect job. I can't preach a perfect sermon. I admit, I am a recovering perfectionist. You can spot a perfectionist because he will tell you he is

---

1. *Merriam-Webster.com Dictionary*, s.v. "perfect," accessed April 7, 2021, https://www.merriam-webster.com/dictionary/perfect.

not a perfectionist. If you struggle in this area, then you will tell someone you don't. We all struggle with this because we want to do a good job. There's a difference between wanting to a good job and wanting to do a perfect job.

He Is Perfect

Here are some Scriptures about this.

> *As for* God, His way *is* perfect;
> The word of the Lord is proven;
> He *is* a shield to all who trust in Him (Psalm 18:30).

> The law of the Lord *is* perfect, converting the soul;
> The testimony of the Lord *is* sure, making wise the simple
> (Psalm 19:7).

> For we do not have a High Priest who cannot sympathize with our weaknesses, but was in all *points* tempted as *we are, yet* without sin (Hebrews 4:15).

This is about Jesus. He lived a perfect life. He has no weaknesses (imperfections) and was without sin (never missed the mark—the center of the bullseye).

The world examined Him and couldn't find a defect. The leader of the world said, "I find no fault in Him." Pilate said this of Jesus three times (John 18:38; 19:4, 6).

I Am Perfected

This is the meat of the message. We are perfected by grace. Perfected in the Father's sight. Without fault or defect.

Matthew 5:48 is a key Scripture about this that is often misapplied:

> Therefore you *shall be perfect,* just as your Father in heaven is perfect (emphasis added).

"Shall be" means you are not perfect now. But Jesus is saying "Once I do on the cross what I have to do, you shall be perfect. Lacking nothing."

The word perfect here is *teleos.* It is an adjective describing a person and means 'complete' or 'finished.' "You will be complete once I complete you."

The verb of this Greek word, *teleo,* is found in John 19:30: "So when Jesus had received the sour wine, He said, 'It is finished!' And bowing His head, He gave up His spirit." This is the same word that is translated 'perfect' in Matthew 5: "The work I did on this cross is perfect. It is done." Because of what Jesus did for us, we have been perfected—made complete.

Jesus was also completed at the cross. To do the complete work he had to be crucified, dead, and buried. In Luke 13:32, after the disciples tell Jesus that Herod is trying to kill Him, Jesus says, "Go, tell that fox, 'Behold, I cast out demons and perform cures today and tomorrow, and the third *day* I shall be perfected.'" Hebrews 5:9 talks about Jesus *having been perfected*. John 17:33 and Hebrews 12:23 speak of how we are *made perfect*. It is the same Greek word.

Hebrews 10:1 says, "For the law, having a shadow of the good things to come, *and* not the very image of the things, can never with these same sacrifices, which they offer continually year by year, make those who approach perfect." The law cannot make perfect those who approach.

Hebrews 7:28 summarizes this. "For the law appoints as high priests men who have weakness, but the word of the oath, which came after the law, *appoints* the Son who has been perfected forever." "Oath" refers to the New Covenant, which came after the law. Jesus is now the High Priest and has been perfected (completed).

Hebrews 10:14 explains how this process works. "For by one offering He has perfected forever those who are being sanctified." Simply put, He has made perfect those who are still imperfect. He has made us perfect in the sight of God.

When it dawns on you that Christ has done everything to make you perfect and complete, you will realize that you don't have to strive to be perfect anymore.

Another way to say this is that I'm not perfect in my behavior, but my belief puts me in a perfect relationship with God. **I'm not perfect by performance, but I am perfect by my position in Christ.**

I have often been good at giving grace to others, but lousy at giving grace to myself. Many of you are the same. I hope you will receive God's grace. That you will learn to not be so hard on yourself because you are striving to attain something you can never attain through your behavior but have already attained through your belief.

Can you receive God's complete and finished grace? Stop trying to be perfect. Be glad that you've been perfected.

NOTES

TALK

These questions can be used for group discussion or personal reflection.

Question 1

Why do you think you might be seeking perfectionism?

Question 2

How does perfectionism exhibit itself in your life?

Question 3

What are the negatives of seeking perfectionism?

Question 4

How does Jesus' perfection shine through our weaknesses and brokenness?

PRAY

If studying alone, ask the Holy Spirit to reveal the truth about Himself to you. If in a group, take some time to pray for each other as you think about the truths discussed in this session.

EXPLORE

Do you want to go deeper with this teaching? Here are some additional things to think about, pray for, or write about in your journal throughout the next week.

Key Quote

> *I'm not perfect in my behavior, but my belief puts me in a perfect relationship with God.*

How can you turn over your needs, desires, and results to the Lord?

____

____

____

____

____

Key Verses

Romans 3:23; Psalm 18:30; Galatians 3:3; Hebrews 4:15; 10:14

What truths stand out to you as you read these verses?

What is the Holy Spirit saying to you through these Scriptures?

Key Question

How does God's grace perfect us?

Key Prayer

Father God, we confess that we are not perfect. But You are! You are perfect in every way: Your way, Your law, Your Son. Fill us with Your Holy Spirit so that we might be made perfect in you. May Your Word, Your truth, and Your Spirit flow out of us to encourage, love, and help others. Draw others to know You through us. In Jesus' name, Amen.

2

STRESSED OUT

Stress has an unexpected purpose in our lives, but how do we deal with it biblically and without breaking?

ENGAGE

What everyday activities do you enjoy that others probably find stressful?

RECAP

In the previous session, we learned that we can never be perfect, and we aren't expected to behave perfectly. We are perfected by God's grace.

Did perfectionism show up in your life this week? If so, how did you deal with it?

WATCH

Watch "Stressed Out."

- Think about the pressures of life that weigh on you.
- Look for how God helps us deal with that pressure.

(If you are not able to watch this teaching on video, read the following. Otherwise, skip to the **Talk** section after viewing.)

READ

Perfectionism is in all of our lives, and it causes all of us extreme stress. Often, the cause of stress is something external. We as believers don't like to hear that we are "stressed out" or under stress. We like to say that we cast all our cares on Jesus because Jesus cares for us. That we don't have stress. But stress is not something you have internally. It's something that comes on you. It's not an insult or an accusation to say you are under stress.

Picture a board stretched between two sawhorses. Now think of different stressors that take place in life, such as a mortgage, job responsibilities, family activities, and so forth. Picture these stressors as weights that are placed on that board. What does it do? That's right, it sags. Then picture even bigger weights: a global pandemic and a presidential election. Place those weights on the board, one after the other, and eventually the board snaps.

There are three things you can do when you're under stress.

Check Your Weights

There are weights on you that you can't remove, but there are also weights that you can remove. Can you take a leave of absence from the PTA? Can you sign up for fewer activities for your children? Some volunteer actions help encourage you, but others might weigh you down. Can you pull something back? You have some weights that you can take off, at least for a season.

Don't put more weights on your board when you are stressed out. Don't take on a new project. It's not just a matter of time management; it's also energy management.

I was asked once, "What do you do when a once-in-a-lifetime opportunity comes along?" I replied, "There is no once-in-a-lifetime opportunity for a believer. It is either God's will, or it isn't." If it is a great opportunity but the wrong season for it, God can bring you back around to it at the right time.

Strengthen Your Board

Strengthen your inner man. Tribulation is guaranteed in this world, but you can increase your training, skill, and preparedness to deal with stresses and opportunities when they come along.

In our illustration earlier, the board we used was a certain thickness. If you put a much thicker board, perhaps made of many boards glued together, you can bear much greater weight. That can be personal friends or the community of believers. Plus, when you get in a strong church, God can give you some God-ideas. All of the inventions that have improved mankind have come from His wisdom.

By taking flat boards, gluing them together, and then turning them on their side, vertically, to make a beam, you can further increase the strength of your board. **We strengthen ourselves by the basics: God's Word, prayer, and worship.** But if you also want to "go from victory to victory," as we often say, remember that you must have a battle to have a victory. You will go from battle to battle. You will have *tribulation* (see John 16:33). This word means outside pressure that hems you in. Romans 5:3–4 says, "Tribulation produces perseverance; and perseverance, character."

Remember that you learn to solve big problems by first solving small problems. You only learn when your brain is aroused. The more stress you have in your life, the more you learn. You must learn how to deal with it.

You have heard about "rising to the challenge." Actually, we all fall to whatever our level of skill, preparation, and training is. The good news is you can do something about those things so that you can be at your desired level.

A while back I had the opportunity to play golf with Jack Nicklaus, who told me that under pressure, everyone reverts to his own swing. Jack tells the story that after 17 years of winning at least two tournaments every year, in 1979 he didn't win one. He went back to his coach and had his coach reteach him the basics. In 1980, he won two majors!

Strengthen your character, because under stress, you will fall back to your level of training. Keep in God's presence, the Word of God, fellowship, and prayer.

Soak Your Board

For centuries, to strengthen a board to prevent it from breaking, people have stressed a board by soaking it in one of two substances: water or oil. Think of it as believers: Water as the Word of God, and oil being the Spirit of God. Worship God in spirit and in truth. It's amazing the shapes boards can be made into by soaking them.

What I miss the most during the COVID-19 pandemic is being with people. Yes, since the pandemic started, Gateway Church has grown by 10,000 members. I don't want you to come back until it is safe and appropriate, but at some point we need to get back together to worship God.

On my sabbatical this summer, God convicted me and reminded me that while resting and not working is important on the Sabbath, *refreshing* is even more important. (I'll need to revise my recent book, *Take the Day Off*, to reflect this.) Exodus 31:17 says that "on the seventh day He rested and was *refreshed*" (emphasis added). I had forgotten how, in addition to resting, I would also spend an extended time in the presence of God. When I confessed this lapse, God gave me a word: "repent." Not what I expected. You may not be able to spend extended time in His presence every day, but you can do so once a week. If you spend extended time in the presence of the Lord, then it will change your life.

NOTES

TALK

These questions can be used for group discussion or personal reflection.

Question 1

What weights are you carrying: job, house, finances, illness, etc.?

____

____

____

____

Question 2

Are there any obligations or stresses you can remove? (For example, get someone to watch your children for a few hours, or take a temporary absence from a volunteer position.)

____

____

____

____

Question 3

How can you strengthen yourself?

Question 4

In Revelation, Jesus tells the church at Ephesus that they have forgotten their first love. How can we go back to the beginning, to the basics of our faith, and find our first love?

PRAY

If studying alone, ask the Holy Spirit to reveal the truth about Himself to you. If in a group, take some time to pray for each other as you think about the truths discussed in this session.

EXPLORE

Do you want to go deeper with this teaching? Here are some additional things to think about, pray for, or write about in your journal throughout the next week.

Key Quote

> *If you spend extended time in the presence of the Lord, then it will change your life.*

What specific action will you take to ensure a regular extended time with the Lord?

Key Verses

1 Peter 5:7; John 4:23; 16:33; Romans 5:3–4

What truths stand out to you as you read these verses?

___

___

___

What is the Holy Spirit saying to you through these Scriptures?

___

___

___

Key Question

How can you "soak your board" this week and grow to a new spiritual level?

Key Prayer

Father God, in these difficult and stressful days, please teach us and mold us into Your likeness. Show us what stresses can be removed from our lives and how to strengthen ourselves in You. Soak us in Your Word and holy presence. May this time make us stronger and more prepared for the next season. May Your people rise up and be a light for the world, leading others to know and love You. In Jesus' name, Amen.

3

GOOD ENOUGH

God's grace far outweighs the good we try to achieve on our own.

ENGAGE

Has there been a home project, a school assignment, or a meal you've prepared where you said, "Well, it's good enough," but it was actually a mess?

RECAP

In the previous session, we learned that we have to manage the things that stress us, and that to absorb the stresses of life we have to strengthen ourselves through God's presence.

Did you make any changes last week to remove unnecessary stressors from your life? How did you strengthen or soak your personal board?

WATCH

Watch "Good Enough."

- Think about how man defines what is good and perfect.
- Look for how the grace of God makes us good enough.

(If you are not able to watch this teaching on video, read the following. Otherwise, skip to the **Talk** section after viewing.)

READ

Like "perfect," the phrase "good enough" has become a catch-phrase, although not with a positive meaning. Like many of us, you may have tried to assemble some furniture or a swing set and ended up thinking, "That's good enough," while in the end having to get help to get it done correctly.

We're going to see that the word good is not a bad word. In the Scripture, if you're not perfect, is it okay if God says you're good? Look at the story of the rich, young ruler.

> Now as He was going out on the road, one came running, knelt before Him, and asked Him, "Good Teacher, what shall I do that I may inherit eternal life?"
>
> So Jesus said to him, "Why do you call Me good? No one *is* good but One, *that is,* God. You know the commandments: 'Do not commit adultery,' 'Do not murder,' 'Do not steal,' 'Do not bear false witness,' 'Do not defraud,' 'Honor your father and your mother.'"
>
> And he answered and said to Him, "Teacher, all these things I have kept from my youth."
>
> Then Jesus, looking at him, loved him, and said to him, "One thing you lack: Go your way, sell whatever you have and give to the poor, and you will have treasure in heaven; and come, take up the cross, and follow Me."
>
> But he was sad at this word, and went away sorrowful, for he had great possessions (Mark 10:17-22).

Notice that the man said he had kept all these commandments. These were the last six commandments, those dealing with our relationship with each other. He could have kept them. The man could not have said that he had kept the other four about man's relationship with God, though.

The focus of the man's question was being good enough. Jesus says to him, in essence, "That's not enough." You can't be good enough to go to heaven. The only way you can go to heaven is to give everything up to God. In other words, to be perfect. This is how God defines good.

Good Is Good

I think we've lost the meaning of the word good. A dictionary list of the meanings for good includes many words: favorable character, bountiful, handsome, attractive, suitable, pleasant, wholesome, amusing, clever, true, honorable ... and at least a dozen more.

Good is not bad: good is good! But we're talking about good or perfect. As an example, is your job good or perfect? One time when I first preached, I had a side job cleaning restrooms. It resulted in a very unpleasant mess one time when I was cleaning a toilet. But it was probably the perfect job for me at the time.

Men, is your wife good or perfect? (The answer is, "Yes!") One time when Debbie and I were having a humorous disagreement, I said to her, "Contrary to popular belief, you are not perfect." She replied, "I'm perfect for you." So my wife is a good wife and a perfect wife. When God gives a gift, it's perfect for us, but it's also a good gift. Good is not bad. Good is good.

Grace Is Good

Watch what happens next in the story in Mark.

> Then Jesus looked around and said to His disciples, "How hard it is for those who have riches to enter the kingdom of God!" And the disciples were astonished at His words. But Jesus answered again and said to them, "Children, how hard it is for those who trust in riches to enter the kingdom of God! It is easier for a camel to go through the eye of a needle than for a rich man to enter the kingdom of God."
>
> And they were greatly astonished, saying among themselves, "Who then can be saved?"
>
> But Jesus looked at them and said, "With men *it is* impossible, but not with God; for with God all things are possible"
> (Mark 10:23-27).

The disciples were *astonished* (meaning 'amazed') at His words. They were *greatly astonished* (a compound word also meaning 'to strike with a blow'). It was like Jesus hit them in the face with amazement. Why were they astonished?

The disciples were not poor, as many people think. When the fisherman disciples left to follow Jesus, they left their *nets* and their *boats* with their *hired servants*. They had employees. Poor people do not have employees. They weren't rich, but they were not poor.

Matthew was a tax collector, and Simon the zealot was a lobbyist (politician). They had money. That's why they were astonished and afraid when they heard Jesus talk about it being hard to get into heaven if you had money. So they asked, "Then who can be saved?" Jesus answered that with men it's impossible. In other words, you can't save yourself. You can't be good enough. You need a Savior—someone who can do it for you.

An acceptable sacrifice to God had to be *perfect*: "And whoever offers a sacrifice of a peace offering to the Lord, to fulfill *his* vow, or a freewill offering from the cattle or the sheep, it must be perfect to be accepted; there shall be no defect in it" (Leviticus 22:21). "Your lamb shall be without blemish, a male of the first year. You may take *it* from the sheep or from the goats" (Exodus 12:5). This was fulfilled in Christ: "With the precious blood of Christ, as of a lamb without blemish and without spot" (1 Peter 1:19).

We've been talking about perfectionism and stress. You'll never overcome perfectionism by doing good or being better. You'll only overcome it by grace. The law (Leviticus and Deuteronomy) has 613 questions. God says, "To go to heaven, you have to get them all correct." And guess what? You've already missed about 600 of them. You've failed.

God's Son, however, has already taken the test and scored a perfect score. God says we can take His score for ourselves and pass and go to heaven, or try to take it even though we've already failed. That should be an easy decision.

Here is the problem with believers: We accept grace, and then we still try to be perfect in everything we do. We're human and will make mistakes, but we are good because God has made us good.

God Is Good

There's a huge anti-God mood online that anticipates your search. Theology online is unreliable. So I put in the search, "Does the word *good* come from God?" Hundreds of articles came back that good is not from God. But all you need is to go to the Bible.

> So you shall rejoice in every good *thing* which the Lord your God has given to you and your house, you and the Levite and the stranger who *is* among you (Deuteronomy 26:11).
>
> Oh, give thanks to the Lord, for *He is* good!
> For His mercy *endures* forever (Psalm 118:1).
>
> You *are* good, and do good;
> Teach me Your statutes (Psalm 119:68).
>
> The Lord *is* good to all,
> And His tender mercies *are* over all His works (Psalm 145:9).
>
> And we know that all things work together for good to those who love God, to those who are the called according to *His* purpose (Romans 8:28).

> For every creature of God *is* good, and nothing is to be refused if it is received with thanksgiving (1 Timothy 4:4).

> Beloved, do not imitate what is evil, but what is good. He who does good is of God, but he who does evil has not seen God (3 John 11).

So let's answer the question. Is good "good enough" if God says it's good? Yes!

God created the world in six days. At the end of each day of Creation, God checked for one thing:

- Day One: Genesis 1:4—"And God saw the light, that it was good."
- Day Two: Genesis 1:10—"And God saw that it was good."
- Day Three: Genesis 1:12—"And God saw that it was good."
- Day Four: Genesis 1:18—"And God saw that it was good."
- Day Five: Genesis 1:21—"And God saw that it was good."

On day six, God created man before He created woman. Genesis 2:18 says that wasn't good (without woman). But at the end of day six, after creating woman, it was *very good*.

Good is good enough with God. It's good enough to be made good by God's grace. You are good enough because you are perfect in your Father's eyes.

NOTES

TALK

These questions can be used for group discussion or personal reflection.

Question 1

What good gifts of God do you have in your life? How is God trying to shape you through these gifts?

Question 2

Have you been trying to earn your way to heaven by being good? Why will that not work?

Question 3

What sin do you need to give up, repent from, and accept God's grace?

Question 4

Do you believe God is good? In all situations and every area of your life? In every struggle?

PRAY

If studying alone, ask the Holy Spirit to reveal the truth about Himself to you. If in a group, take some time to pray for each other as you think about the truths discussed in this session.

EXPLORE

Do you want to go deeper with this teaching? Here are some additional things to think about, pray for, or write about in your journal throughout the next week.

Key Quote

> *Here is the problem with believers: We accept grace, and then we still try to be perfect in everything we do.*

How can you accept God's grace to know that you are good?

____

____

____

____

____

Key Verses

Mark 10:17–27; James 1:17

What truths stand out to you as you read these verses?

___

___

___

What is the Holy Spirit saying to you through these Scriptures?

___

___

___

Key Question

How can you be good without being perfect?

Key Prayer

Father, we thank You for Your goodness! You are good—*always*. We thank You for your amazing Son, who was perfect in every way and sacrificed Himself for our benefit. Father, we pray for those who need Your grace to come into agreement with You and find peace through believing in Your Son, our Savior. In Jesus' name, Amen.

4

SIMPLY HUMAN

We are not super-human or sub-human. We are simply human, perfected through Jesus.

ENGAGE

If you could pick one super-human characteristic, what would it be and why?

RECAP

In the previous session, we learned that God is good, and through His grace we can find healing and redemption.

What examples did you see at work in your life this week of the goodness of God?

WATCH

Watch "Simply Human."

- Think about what it means to be super-human or sub-human.
- Look for how God's grace allows us to be simply human.

(If you are not able to watch this teaching on video, read the following. Otherwise, skip to the **Talk** section after viewing.)

READ

We'll look at some terms that some of you may think don't relate to you, but you will see that the concepts relate to all of us. Those terms are super-human, sub-human, and simply human.

Most of us would say we don't think of ourselves as super-human. Then why do you keep taking on more than you should? Or we wouldn't think of ourselves as sub-human, but then why do you keep beating yourself up? This is something God has been dealing with me about for a long time.

Our Scripture for this message is Philippians 2:5–8:

> Think of yourselves the way Christ Jesus thought of himself. He had equal status with God but didn't think so much of himself that he had to cling to the advantages of that status no matter what. Not at all. When the time came, he set aside the privileges of deity and took on the status of a slave, became *human*! Having become human, he stayed human. It was an incredibly humbling process. He didn't claim special privileges. Instead, he lived a selfless, obedient life and then died a selfless, obedient death—and the worst kind of death at that—a crucifixion (MSG).

We Are Not Super-human

Look at verse 6. If there ever was a superman, it was Jesus. He had equal status with God, yet He didn't "cling to the advantages of that status." Jesus was super. He's not from this world. He could fly (ascended into heaven in Acts 1). He walked on water and raised dead people. He was human, and He stayed human. He had power and authority, but He only used His power and authority to help people.

Luke 5:16 says that Jesus went into the wilderness and prayed. Jesus knew He was human and needed prayer.

Matthew 4:2 says Jesus was hungry after fasting for 40 days and nights. Humans get hungry after fasting.

In Matthew 8:24, Jesus was asleep on the boat during the storm. Humans sleep.

Jesus ate when He was hungry, He slept when He was tired, and He withdrew from busyness to pray. Jesus lived as a human.

Philippians 2:5 says, "Think of yourselves the way Christ Jesus thought of Himself." And Jesus thought of Himself as a human.

I think we commit too much. We say yes to too many things. We think somehow that we can be super-human. We overcommit and we overwork.

On Easter weekend in 2012, we added a sunrise service to our Easter program. At that time I still spoke live at every service. I delivered two sermons on Friday, three on Saturday, and four on Sunday. Speaking like that is draining. Then on Monday I flew to Australia and spoke in several conferences for over a week. By the next Monday I had developed a bleeding ulcer and was hospitalized. I thought I was super-human, but I quickly found out that I was not.

We Are Not Sub-human

Verse 7 in this passage says that Jesus took on the status of a slave and became human. But even though He became human and came to serve, He never struggled with being a Son. When Satan tempted Jesus, he said, "If You are the Son of God ..." Jesus never argued that point with Satan because He was secure in the knowledge of His Sonship. The main reason we tend to feel sub-human or less than others, is that we feel we are less than a son or daughter of God. All sons and all daughters are equal before God.

We tend to look at our performance. I've always had a problem with feeling "less than." Even after 40 years being saved, the enemy still reminds me of my past.

Remember the story of the Pharisee and the prostitute (see Luke 7:36–50). The prostitute wets the feet of Jesus with her tears and dries His feet with her hair. The Pharisee was thinking, *If only He knew who was touching Him*. The woman thought she was sub-human. The Pharisee thought he was super-human. Jesus taught a parable that said, "You are both the same." They were both lacking when it comes to the Father. They were lacking in the exact same amount.

There's a Pharisee and a prostitute in all of us. There are times when we think we are better than others. People who aren't like us. We try to avoid that thought, but it's there. And there are times we think we are worse than others. But we are not super-human or sub-human. We are all on the same level. **We are all broken humans in need of God's grace.**

The problem is not how we see others. The problem is how we see ourselves. You know what you struggle with, but you don't know what others struggle with.

We Are Simply Human

So what does it mean to just be a human? Look again at Philippians 2:8:

> He didn't claim special privileges. Instead, he lived a selfless, obedient life and then died a selfless, obedient death—and the worst kind of death at that—a crucifixion (MSG).

It's right there: *To live a selfless, obedient life and die a selfless, obedient death*. Even crucifixion. In other words, die to self.

Jesus had a cross, but He also says we are to take up our cross. We are to take it up every day.

So for me to be human means that I'm going to make mistakes. I'm not going to beat myself up. I'm going to allow myself to make mistakes. I'm not going to strive for perfection. I'm just going to trust that I'm a human.

Guilt and shame take more Christians out than sin. Because it's the way we think of ourselves. If you're ever going to overcome any weakness or any sin, it's only going to be overcome through grace.

Moses took up two full chapters of the Bible, out of 1,189, arguing with God.

> Moses objected, "They won't trust me. They won't listen to a word I say. They're going to say, 'God? Appear to him? Hardly!'" (Exodus 4:1 MSG).
>
> Moses raised another objection to God: "Master, please, I don't talk well. I've never been good with words, neither before nor after you spoke to me. I stutter and stammer" (v. 10 MSG).
>
> He said, "O my Lord, please send by the hand of whomever *else* You may send" (v. 13 MSG).

And my favorite:

> But Moses said to God, "Who *am* I that I should go to Pharaoh, and that I should bring the children of Israel out of Egypt?" (3:11 MSG).

God's answer in essence was, "Who are you?! What matters is who *I AM!*" Remember, God told Moses to tell the people "I AM" sent you. *"All you need to do is carry a stick and pick it up when I tell you to. I can part the Red Sea. I can turn water into blood. I can do it all, Moses. I just need you to show up! I can take care of it."*

I work with a consultant who is also a psychologist. I talk with him about every insecure thought. A few years ago I told him I wanted to talk about how people see me. (He said he'd also been wanting to talk with me about that.)

I explained that some people don't know me at all. Some people see me as a pastor. Some people see me as a pastor of a large, influential church. But some people see me as a famous person or even as a celebrity, and that's a problem.

The consultant said that's something we needed to dive into—at our next session, since it will take a while and we were almost out of time. Of course, we meet only once every three months!

When we got back together, I wanted to start where we left off last time. I was very animated about it. I said I had a problem with how I perceive people see me. How does that affect me? Why does that matter? His answer: "It doesn't matter." I thought, *That's all? That's what I waited three months for?*

> He said, "It only matters how God sees you and how you see yourself." Then he asked, "How does God see you?"
> "He sees me as perfect."
> "And how do you see you?"
> "Extremely flawed."
> He said, "That's why this is going to take a while to talk about this."

Don't try to be super-human. Don't think of yourself as less than human. You're simply human—and that's good enough for God.

NOTES

TALK

These questions can be used for group discussion or personal reflection.

Question 1

Pastor Robert discussed the different ways we strive for perfection. Which aspect of being human do you struggle with most?

Question 2

Why is it easier to think of ourselves as sub-human or super-human instead of simply human?

Question 3

Read Philippians 2:5–8. Why do you think the Bible says we are to think of ourselves the way Jesus thought of Himself?

Question 4

How do you see yourself?

Question 5

How does God see you?

PRAY

If studying alone, ask the Holy Spirit to reveal the truth about Himself to you. If in a group, take some time to pray for each other as you think about the truths discussed in this session.

EXPLORE

Do you want to go deeper with this teaching? Here are some additional things to think about, pray for, or write about in your journal throughout the next week.

Key Quote

There's a Pharisee and a prostitute in all of us.

In what way do you identify with the person of the Pharisee? The prostitute?

____

____

____

____

____

Key Verses

Philippians 2:5-8; Ephesians 3:11

What truths stand out to you as you read these verses?

What is the Holy Spirit saying to you through these Scriptures?

Key Question

Will you accept God's grace and see yourself as He sees you?

Key Prayer

Heavenly Father, thank You for being such a good Father to us. Thank You for the grace You give. Help us rest in Your completed work. May we embrace the truth that we are not perfect humans, but we have been perfected by the cross. Help us rest in Your grace. In Jesus' name, Amen.

LEADER'S GUIDE

The *Perfect or Perfected* Leader's Guide is designed to help you lead your small group or class through the *Perfect or Perfected* curriculum. Use this guide along with the curriculum for a life-changing, interactive experience.

BEFORE YOU MEET

- Ask God to prepare the hearts and minds of the people in your group. Ask Him to show you how to encourage each person to integrate the principles all of you discover into your daily lives through group discussion and writing in your journals.
- Preview the video segment for the week.
- Plan how much time you'll give to each portion of your meeting (see the suggested schedule below). In case you're unable to get through all of the activities in the time you have planned, here is a list of the most important questions (from the **Talk** section) for each week.

SESSION ONE

Q: How does perfectionism exhibit itself in your life?

Q: What are the negatives of seeking perfectionism?

SESSION TWO

Q: What weights are you carrying: job, house, finances, illness, etc.?

Q: How can you strengthen yourself?

SESSION THREE

Q: What good gifts of God do you have in your life? How is God trying to shape you through these gifts?

Q: Have you been trying to earn your way to heaven by being good? Why will that not work?

SESSION FOUR

Q: How do you see yourself?

Q: How does God see you?

SUGGESTED SCHEDULE

1. **Engage** and **Recap** (5 Minutes)
2. **Watch** or **Read** (20 Minutes)
3. **Talk** (25 Minutes)
4. **Pray** (10 minutes)

HOW TO USE THE CURRICULUM

The One Thing

This is a brief statement under each session title that sums up the main point—the key idea—of the session.

Engage

Ask the icebreaker question to help get people talking and feeling comfortable with one another.

Recap

At the first meeting, provide an overview of the curriculum and encourage everyone to read and prepare before each meeting. For the following meetings, recap the previous session and invite members to talk about any opportunities they have encountered to apply what they learned.

Watch

Watch the videos (recommended).

Read

If you're unable to watch the videos, read these sections.

Talk

The questions in this curriculum are intentionally open-ended. Use them to help the group members reflect on Scripture and the truths learned in the session.

Pray

Ask members to share their concerns and then pray together. Be sensitive to the Holy Spirit and the needs of the group.

Explore

Encourage members to complete the written portion in their books before the next meeting.

KEY TIPS FOR THE LEADER

- Generate participation and discussion.
- Resist the urge to teach. The goal is for great conversation that leads to discovery.
- Ask open-ended questions—questions that can't be answered with "yes" or "no" (e.g., "What do you think about that?" rather than "Do you agree?")
- When a question arises, ask the group for their input first, instead of immediately answering it yourself.
- Be comfortable with silence. If you ask a question and no one responds, rephrase the question and wait for a response. Your primary role is to create an environment where people feel comfortable to be themselves and participate, not to provide the answers to all of their questions.
- Ask the group to pray for each other from week to week, especially about key issues that arise during your group time. This is how you begin to build authentic community and encourage spiritual growth within the group.

KEYS TO A DYNAMIC SMALL GROUP

Relationships

Meaningful, encouraging relationships are the foundation of a dynamic small group. Teaching, discussion, worship, and prayer are important elements of a group meeting, but the depth of each element is often dependent upon the depth of the relationships among members.

Availability

Building a sense of community within your group requires members to prioritize their relationships with one another. This means being available to listen, care for one another, and meet each other's needs.

Mutual Respect

Mutual respect is shown when members value each other's opinions (even when they disagree) and are careful never to put down or embarrass others in the group (including their spouses, who may or may not be present).

Openness

A healthy small group environment encourages sincerity and transparency. Members treat each other with grace in areas of weakness, allowing each other room to grow.

Confidentiality

To develop authenticity and a sense of safety within the group, each member must be able to trust that things discussed within the group will not be shared outside the group.

Shared Responsibility

Group members will share the responsibility of group meetings by using their God-given abilities to serve at each gathering. Some may greet, some may host, some may teach, etc. Ideally, each person should be available to care for others as needed.

Sensitivity

Dynamic small groups are born when the leader consistently seeks and is responsive to the guidance of the Holy Spirit, following His leading throughout the meeting as opposed to sticking to the "agenda." This guidance is especially important during the discussion and ministry time.

Fun!

Dynamic small groups take the time to have fun. Create an atmosphere for fun and be willing to laugh at yourself every now and then!

ABOUT THE AUTHOR

Robert Morris is the senior pastor of Gateway Church, a multi-campus church based in the Dallas/Fort Worth Metroplex. Since it began in 2000, the church has grown to more than 100,000 active attendees. His television program airs in over 190 countries, and his radio program, *Worship & the Word* with Pastor Robert, airs in more than 1,800 radio markets across America. He serves as chancellor of The King's University and is the bestselling author of numerous books, including *The Blessed Life*, *Frequency*, *Beyond Blessed*, and *Take the Day Off*. Robert and his wife, Debbie, have been married 41 years and are blessed with one married daughter, two married sons, and nine grandchildren.

NOTES